GW00373019

Piano
Grade 3

Pieces & Exercises
for Trinity College London
examinations

2012-2014

Published by
Trinity College London

Registered Office:
4th floor, 89 Albert Embankment
London SE1 7TP UK

T +44 (0)20 7820 6100
F +44 (0)20 7820 6161
E music@trinitycollege.co.uk
www.trinitycollege.co.uk

Registered in the UK
Company no. 02683033
Charity no. 1014792

Printed in England by Halstan Printing Group, Amersham, Bucks.

Polonaise

BWV Anh. 128 from *Notebook for Anna Magdalena*

Anonymous

Dynamics are editorial.

Sonatina

HWV 585

George Frideric Handel
(1685-1759)

Dynamics and articulation are editorial.

Menuett in F

K. 5

Wolfgang Amadeus Mozart
(1756-1791)

Dynamics are editorial.

The repeats should be played in the examination and candidates are encouraged to vary the dynamics the second time.

Pastorale

op. 100 no. 3

Johann Burgmüller
(1806-1874)

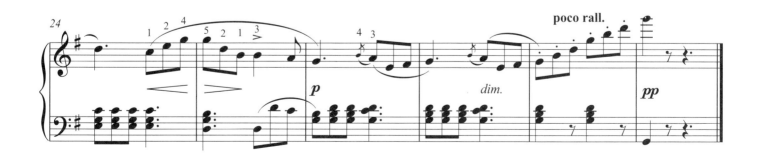

Romance

Felix Mendelssohn
(1809-1847)

Requiem for a Little Bird

Gustave Sandré
(1843-1916)

Bange Frage (Anxious Question)

no. 8 from *Aus der Jugendzeit* op. 17

Max Reger
(1873-1916)

Song of Twilight

Yoshinao Nakada

The repeat should be played in the examination.
Composer's metronome mark ♩ = **60**.

Jazzy Joey

Catherine Rollin

Exercises

1a. Keeping One's Balance – tone, balance and voicing

1b. A Little Off-beat – tone, balance and voicing

2a. Mountain Mists – co-ordination

2b. Up Hill and Down – co-ordination

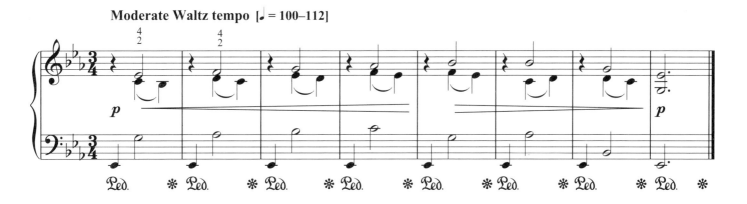

3a. Over and Under – finger & wrist strength and flexibility

3b. Nimble Jack – finger & wrist strength and flexibility

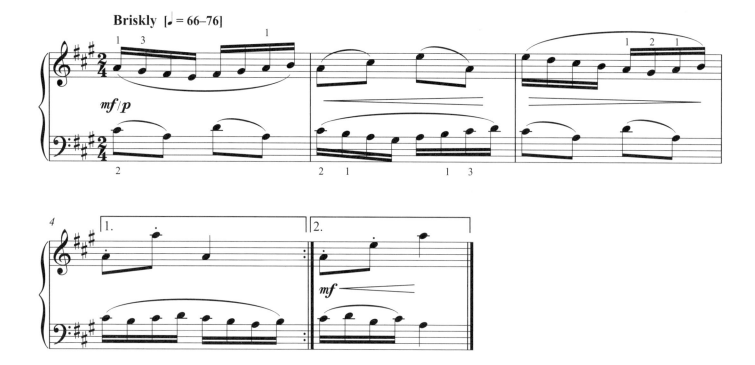

The repeat should be played in the examination.